Stepmommy!

Written and Illustrated by Libby Tyree

To Oree and Papa Brock, with love.

Hi! I have a stepmommy!

That means I have two kinds of mommies.

One is my mommy.

She looks like me.

My mommy lives at mommy's house.

Mommy's house is my house too.

I love my mommy!
She loves me too!

My other kind of mommy is my stepmommy.

My stepmommy and my daddy live at daddy's house.

Daddy's house is my house too.

My stepmommy takes care of daddy and me.

My stepmommy is just like other mommies.

She makes me yummy lunch.

We all go to the beach together.

My stepmommy reads books to me.

She helps daddy tuck me in at night.

We do silly dances together!

My stepmommy takes me shopping.

We play hide and seek!

She helps me do arts and crafts.

My stepmommy teaches me how to make castles!

She takes me to the pool.

We go to the park to play with my friends!

I love my stepmommy!

She loves me too!

A picture of my stepmommy and me!

www.ingramcontent.com/pod-product-compliance
Lightning Source LLC
Chambersburg PA
CBHW042130040426
42450CB00003B/134